RINA

Rina's War

Julian Stannard

PETERLOO POETS

First published in 2001
by Peterloo Poets
The Old Chapel, Sand Lane, Calstock, Cornwall PL18 9QX, U.K.

© 2001 by Julian Stannard

**A catalogue record for this book is available
from the British Library**

ISBN 1-871471-93-1

Printed in Great Britain By
Antony Rowe Ltd, Chippenham, Wilts.

ACKNOWLEDGEMENTS

London Magazine, Ambit, Stand, Poetry Ireland Review, Thumbscrew, Verse, The North, Smiths Knoll, Staple, Poetry and Audience, Outposts, Seam, The Frogmore Papers, The Swansea Review, Envoi, Spokes, Quartz, The New Writer, The Crabbe Memorial Anthologies 1996-9, Quaderni Del Dipartimento Di Lingue E Letterature Straniere Moderne Università Di Genova, The East Anglian Daily Times.

'Rina's War' and 'Saint Anna's Funicular' appeared in the Faber anthology *First Pressings*.

'Ballo' received a prize in the 1998 National Poetry Competition. From 1996-1999 Julian Stannard was the holder of the Crabbe Memorial Prize.

southwest arts

Genova dove non vivo…

(Giorgio Caproni 1912-90)

To Cristina, Jack and William

Contents

Lives

Every morning you show me your breasts
and then dissolve into the fog.
This is the way we live our lives:
fleeting moments of human presence
and then the bushes, the woods,
the ineluctable process of weather itself.

Sweets

Vapours from *Trebor*
sweeten the Chesterfield air
then break across the borough's twisted spine.
These travels in a fateful aether...

This was the gateway to heaven
where knee-chapped, hysterical and thin
we caught the train to London
ten-year-old wide boys with *Number Six*
then later came gently back
with sherbet and love-chants...

Mr. Pandya

Mr. Pandya, palmist, poet, swimming instructor
does not, as a rule, suffer from bad colds.

Pandya – Pandy to his friends
came down from London with soft brown hands

pool-deep eyes and a handful of palmistry diplomas.
Describing himself as a mistake

'somewhere between man and woman'
Mr. Pandya announced several startling facts.

Bob's Coat

I inherited a coat.
Early 60's, *Burton's*, weighty
as massive as death itself.
It climbed out of the grave
and wrestled onto me.
I wear it to frighten myself
to frighten the elements.
Or when I'm lonely:
to feel you clinging
onto my back, like a pyramid.

The Apprentice

The butcher's boy knows mostly
two smiles: the chicken and the beef
as he wedges himself into
the hearts of the villagers
doling out pieces of offal
to the careless who mismanaged
their pensions and shouldering
a roast for the blowzy housewife
who drives the capacious Volvo.

All day the pink-cheeked smiles
and the chafed thighs
his apprentice knife swinging up
and down in breathless sculpture
dismemberment before our eyes...
The wiped apron, the Queen's head
curled in blood-tipped fingers.

Like dog-owners, butchers begin
to resemble their favourite cuts.
But the butcher's boy is virginal:
Monday, he's nervous fowl, by Friday
he beefs it up. At so young an age
he could become any meat he chooses.

Saturday, he strips for the deep soak
and lies in troubled waters.
It's quite a ritual: the hot water,
Aphrodite rising from the foam
the soap bar soft and alien
in his tenderizing fingers.
He produces his own thin gravy,
grasps the *charcuterie*
smiles the pork smile, then comes.

Chet Baker

Chet Baker coos baby to sleep
and I stand swinging my hips
just a little too frenetically,
I hope baby doesn't become a torpedo.

We are not in Berlin
nor are we running across *Trastevere*
at five o'clock in the morning
with a brioche hanging out of our mouths,

we are in Ipswich, England.
It has rained for several days.
The milkman's late with his delivery.
Baby was late too, but oh much blessed!

Bawdsey

There would have been a morning like this.
A near empty manor on the edge of the sea
and the waves instructed to be furious.
There would have been a few maids thrashing
cushions and preparing for the visit
that would transcend all previous visits.
The butler would insist on being lame.

There would be gulls liberated by winds
soaring above the punished trees
and the rain would scatter across the lawns.
There would be a fire reticent with its flames
and footsteps bringing a silver tray
to a seated man who possessed a revolver.
There would be more terrible news of the war.

There would be a little courtesy and
the perfume of something rare and leathery.
The old gardener would be truly soaked
and chatter, *sotto voce*, to his private demons.
A horse would rear up in a fit of madness
and the cook would weep all over the dough.
Young men of the estate were suddenly beautiful.

1919

The restaurant was empty, the pale, malarial waiter
brought us a woodcock that fared only a little better

and when he uncorked the hoary wine all the tensions
of the Great War sighed out like afternoon sleep.

We drank a liquid that was as dark as blood
and our thoughts were all tangled in strife,

out hill-top enemy, our murderous mountain-brothers...
The old Duke spoke to his ruddy-eyed wife

who was as deaf as the little dog at their feet
who yelped every time they stood on its paws.

Aldeburgh

The whole house had swept out
to some mediocre ballet in London
and the place was so quiet
we wondered if we were dead.

So you fell back on that old favourite:
Aldeburgh 'out of season' –
a time for ghosts and so bracing
we couldn't open our mouths.

Walking is what the English do
when they have a crisis and you
hardly needed an icy wind
to remind you of spiralling debts.

*We've all been allocated a room
in the Marshalsea,* somebody said,
his cheque book kinder than his heart.
But this was more Dostoesvky than Dickens.

We all brimmed with desperation
and somehow felt better for it
as if by touching the proverbial
rock-bottom we had fulfilled

yet another of our secret wishes.
The bookshop was firmly shut
but there was a room full of bric-à-brac
trying to pass itself off as antiques.

Scarecrows

They drift in from lonely farmsteads
tired of drunken farmers
the relentlessness of the weather
the high spirits of country children

exhausted by crows

they gather on the lawns of the mansion
a quiet assembly of the meek and forsaken.
Some have managed bicycles
others are foot weary
exasperated by wing feathers

without ale.

Many lie on the grass like trench soldiers
pleased at the discovery.
Others affect a dandyish air with yellow cloth
sharpening their hedge-torn coats.

They don't want charity.

Lines on the Turtle

Smell of impending rain, markets, beasts
a late afternoon in the distant past
the Chinese covering their heads with paper
the turtles dead but alive, the chickens
soon to be headless, I think they know.

There's a gaggle of boys in white vests
chasing a frog that hops through the stalls.
There's much laughter, much shouting.
Maybe the frog got away, still hopping
still vaguely pursued by thin hysterical men.

The eggs are well over a hundred years old
and we're still queuing for snake ends.
Mum employs her perpetual present simple
the imperial voice, then barters her way
through a collection of ill-fed captives.

The white woman with the straw hat is
leading her young ones through a rain that
is gathering above the lion mountains
and waiting to burst like a dragon
which has lost patience with its people.

Odours of the East on hot tarmac, the boy
who learnt his English tenses, the past
the unproven future, now moves to French
as he sells his durian fruit to the *gweilos*.
One day he'll become a man and sell souls

on the brutal Borse of his forefathers.
How many lean animals did we eat, waiting
for the rains? This time luckier
than serpents, slow-dying turtles, *poulets*
we cling to our passports, our memories.

The Party

The last flight out of the city.
The bombs were already
dismantling the suburbs...
They wanted the city centre for themselves.

I took a walk downtown
to see how the city's last loyal shopkeepers
were faring with a dying clientele.
And then, unexpectedly, the party.

A party for those who already knew,
years and years and years ago,
they would never have the right papers
for the last flight out of the city.

Erasure

All day now the helicopter
has been hovering over the city
oppressing its citizens and
reminding us all that crimes
will have to be paid for.
Even those surreptitious ones.

I know that somewhere
in the warren that is our neighbourhood
someone is trying to make themselves
invisible, is feeling the sweat
massing at the back of their neck.

Every minute is like a life-time
and they will be thinking just how
wonderful it would be if they
could just fling open the door and
walk down the street, like so.

Exile

Even *il Duce* himself
couldn't have conceived
an internal exile so fraught
with mortifications…

My new land is full of
Methodism and small churches,
a dampness that overwhelms.

Most of the houses are empty
and I am forcing myself
to appreciate the
silence of sheep,
the way the old have learnt
patience, especially
the way a dog never comes
when you call for it…

Via Garibaldi

Last night I dreamed
I walked down *Via Garibaldi*.
The palaces sighed, edging a little closer
and the street was full of turning faces:
of friends now dead, of creditors,
of bloated landlords, of lovers too.
It was difficult to walk through
so many people, difficult to know how best
to face the past. I smiled, I wept,
I bled in several places.

The eyes of some were terrible,
whilst others had hardly changed at all,
my hands were shaken and shaking.
I suppose I was searching for something
at the end of *Via Garibaldi,*
I guess I wanted something as it once was –
But if dreams were made for anything
they were made to confuse and deceive
and I woke, a thousand miles away.

Albion

You have become a little wizened
your hair has become very white.
I should say you were proud of it,
watching your hair turning white.

I wanted to look you in the eyes
and say a few things about myself.
But how do you talk to a man
with a thousand ghosts on his head?

Obsessions

All that winter Rina carefully nursed her two obsessions:
a hateful lack of chicory and the bizarre absence of *bidets*.
At the drop of a hat I found myself speeding off
to some distant cure-all supermarket hoping
for a windfall of chicory. All that winter
we spoke of *bidets*, a comforting place for Rina
to place her large, if tender, continental bottom.

The Journey

Imagine esplanades of steps
that carve their way through

the midriffs of an edifice.
Imagine yourself taking

that route into the viscera
of a lungless palace.

You come to these glassy steps
on a daily basis

which take you surely to a desk
and worse, much worse.

But between the security man
who wants to ruin you

and the *surveillant*
who has taken account

of your usefulness
there are exactly 90 seconds

of windowless ascent
in which you are beholden

to nothing other than
the patina of dust

you scatter into every corner
but slowly, slowly.

The Return

Genoa

It wasn't a dream.

We could see the lighthouse,
all the paraphernalia of the docks
as we lurched out of one tunnel
into another. Light penetrating
darkness. All the black beautiful ships
we had brooded over for years
still lingering in the waters.

We would throw open our shutters
to an applause of possibilities
but the heat forced our hand
and we scuttled into the shadows.
We did not cross the Ligurian water.

For too long we were holed up
in a city that drowned us.
The elderly were too many,
too many hearts on too many sleeves.
How we were hacked to pieces!

The House of Lucia

I travel three continents
before I arrive at the house of Lucia.
Finally when I break through
the sweat barrier
on the eighth floor
and open Lucia's heavy, impressive door
I find *Neve* the cat
looking hungry, confused.
'You don't look a bit like Edouardo!'

At the Flat of Maurizio and Irene

(Sampierdarena)

Marble for my feet
and the train-rock for sleep.
Jut out the shutters
for a flood of light.

Do you remember
the family dog
hanging its head out
of the back of the Zodiac
its lolling tongue
occasionally in repose
against the back
of your tanned neck?

Last night
you showed us
photos of the partisans:
some were arm-wrestling
some were very young,
some were floating
from posts.

Sottoripa

(1984)

I wanted the meanest zone
in the city, so I took a room in
the *Sottoripa* and lived with
a Persian for six heady months.
He fed me on pistachio nuts
the only thing mamma knew how to send
then boasted about his muscles.

Breakfast was a trip downstairs
coffee followed by grappa followed by coffee
a room full of lined stomachs,
the small fry of the criminal class.
There was much talk about nothing
and life was full of throat-cutting gestures.

If you wanted sex you had to pay for it
or wait until the smallest hours.
The Tunisians were always ready to oblige.
Meanwhile the ships drifted
into port to unload their human cargo
and the dogs in the *Sottoripa* multiplied.

San Siro

The priests were calling out for garments
so I climbed into the family heirloom
otherwise known as Bob's coat
my own anti-nuclear defence system
and walked slowly to the church of *San Siro*
where Father Benjamin held both my shoulders
and then blessed the coat
with his strong catholic elbow movements
I could feel the holy water on my face
and then he disabused me of the coat
hauling it away from my body
startling a discreet veiled lady
as he dragged it down the aisle of God
towards the altar and the cross,
I thought for a terrible moment
he was going to use it to mop up the blood
of the naked Christ and I stood
aghast under baroque extravagance
particles of gold-leaf drifting in the light
exquisite landings on the tongue.

The Bay

Here we are in the soft bay of the picture postcard
the bay which is ever-full of illusions –
where the cactus is never really dangerous
and where nearby Lord Byron plunged himself
into the smooth water and swam for hours.
I think he was trying to drown himself
(out of exasperation!) This is the land of the villa!

Here the land has been sipping the sea for centuries
and whole wealthy generations have lived and died
unaware of the meaning of hunger or humiliation
(even death, like lobsters, has been put on ice);
minds have been made jelly by sheer comfort and ease.
Stories of the city disturb and terrify and here
the people vote with all their might for privilege.

A worker, a poor man, are rare unknown breeds
antipatico and will not take root in this warm soil.
Their piazzas are made for sitting and seeing
life is a long, slow, pleasurable drowning,
even the winds taste of pine kernels and basil.
If anyone here had to think too hard
the whole scene might explode before their eyes.

Restoration

(Via Scurreria)

The old woman lived in the house for years…
She climbed these stairs, cooked frugal meals
was without family, had few friends and
a past which had been forgotten by everyone
(perhaps even herself): a past where the radio
was still something of an event
where the voice of the *Duce* boomed into
dark rooms of saints and virgins and spoke
of another Roman Empire to an incredulous
but occasionally proud race that was often more
worried about eking out a living and didn't want life
to be complicated by war and bloodshed.
And some of the stories that seeped through
about their friends the Germans shocked to the bone
and cannot be repeated. Maybe the old woman
had known of someone who disappeared in the night?
- Now millions of lire have been spent to eliminate
every trace of *her*. Every modern gadget's been put in.
The house has a clean, eighties chic full of
thin Italian lamps which bend like anorexic giraffes
and which cause a shine that no old ghost
could possibly survive. All efforts to scrub out
the past have been almost entirely successful…

Oil and Geese

for Eiléan Ni Chuilleanáin

When the krauts left
they took everything with them
so we hurried into the cellar
to cherish our large jar of oil
the oil we use to wash our
kidneys, liver, pancreas, viscera
the oil that pulls us through,
only to find that a mouse
had somehow found a way in
and lay on its back *purée.*
So when the Americans arrived
with cries of *okay, okay**
we had to say that even
the geese had flown away.

*oche is the Italian for geese.

Cari Spazzini

The refuse collectors' strike, 13th November 1992, Genoa.

Cari spazzini, I want you to know
that as far as we're concerned you
can expect the handshake of solidarity.
We know how much the city depends

on your unglamorous sweeping of
the streets. In fact just look
at them now. Everywhere slagheaps
of refuse, food for the rats

their families. Perhaps (strictly,
you understand, between you and us)
we could come to an agreement.
In simple terms: when no one else

is around, you come and clear
that hell-heap outside our house
(after all, we're clean, reasonable people),
we'll continue with that solidarity.

San Giuliano

Genoa

There's an old bar and a hut
and a few tables and little else
that's elegant about the beach
of *San Giuliano*, and little that's
good about the people who go there.
I think I might walk there.

But how I remember the storm.
It was sudden and merciless
and we huddled into a flimsy hut
listening to the rain drenching the tin

roof and the waves crashing against
the flinty, aggrieved sands.
We sort of opened our mouths
and cared about nothing.

Combinations

Although the city had many failings
it had many exquisite bars
but they only existed if you wished them
and were always in the secret places.

So they had to be conjured up,
an intangible combination of
wood, mirrors, memory...

One such place frequently presented itself
and I would hide for days at a time,
it was like breathing behind glass.

Via Mascherona

The sun was strong enough
to break a back.
Dogs slept in the alleys
and no one would wake them
with a kiss...
So why had I come
to these cruel backstreets
when I knew your shutters
would stay shut?
I slipped into the
Bar des Arabes to chase
an inch of coffee
around my mouth.
I shouted up,
the shutter shuddered
but no one spoke.

Vico Casana

How good
to see the tripe shop,
a legacy of
medieval butchery.
Soziglia was once
the city's abattoir.
How it made
my stomach retch,
those cold mornings
before dawn.
So I hurry past,
a little slower,
a strange, suddenly
odourless pleasure.

Cicale

(Salità della Posta Vecchia)

This must be something like hell.
As familiar as a fishmonger's,
this moving tray of fresh *cicale*.
Come, they're cheap. Take some
hell home. You won't get better.

Some are wise enough to be dead.
The rest are arching their thin limbs.
The rest are pleading for water.
They have the most beautiful eyes.

To die alone is more dignified.
But to die like this with so many others!

Shutters

Close the shutters, open the shutters, arrange the shutters
we were delighted with the ritual of our green Genoese shutters
we studied the relationship between light and shutters.
Suddenly the room became a fantasy of sunbeams.
But here come our elderly relatives afraid of the sun
so let us again close the shutters, let us have darkness.

Gorleri

(1992)

1.
Those olives were my eyes...
My vision is the land falling
down to the sea, falling away
from the world. Red roofs
are part of our diet and
the cluster of life around
the church is where my soul
leads when the sun shines,

the fruit grows. The priest
died years ago but still manages
to sing the mass, still knows
the best ways to please God.
The small fires that burn across
the valley are strange communications
and the scent of burning wood
is what we have for breakfast.

They built the motorway
to remind us of death and the
distant roar of the traffic
makes the crickets leap and leap
but does not slow the strawberry
grape that buries us, does not
rifle through our damp cellars,
does not drag us into the light.

2.
Each village built like a fort
to have a wide view of the sea

each village self-contained
with a spire to raise the eyes
olive trees to provide a living
chat to take place in the squares
the terraces womb-like with basil.

On market days the long walk
to sell food, exchange news
weary feet may be bathed in the sea
scallywags swim out to the rocks
carved niches to provide a home
for the virgin mothers of God
the altars piquant with flowers.

When the storms come, panic
the dogs jitter like the possessed
all of us cower in our beds
first we batten down the shutters
children asleep across our knees
sometimes comfort, sometimes tears.
Tomorrow the sun will *surge, surge.*

3.
I dreamed
I was in the piazza of *Gorleri.*

Old Mama Rina walked slowly
into the sunlight

surrounded by chickens.

She sat on her favourite stone
and started the lamentations.

And there was music
a band of bazookas and rockets.

They were carrying an effigy:
Saint Nicolà the village protector.

The dead priest led the procession.
He was daubed in splendour.

I heard *Giorgio* turn to the priest,
'You need a little wind under your cloaks.'

Oh it was a miracle! It was a *festa*!

4.
The blue church of *Gorleri*.

They hired an ecclesiastical artist
who sprayed the inner walls *celeste*.
This was 1863-1887.

The church façade's a slab of pastry
where dogs hover and pant.
The green bells are nearly perfect.

You'll have to imagine the *celeste:*
the doors are always locked
unless you catch the priest, who's dead.

5.
Surprised by their own age
the uncles took out the battered *Fiat*
and drove up into the hills
to see the new baby. They were determined.

Their movements across the piazza slow:
zia Severina with her stick and myopia
zio Nirlo with the cough
that was soon to carry him off.

6.

il gatto

In the afternoon of the village
an afternoon giving space to dreams
fallen leaves of bougainvillaea
sweep through the dusty streets
and a young, skeletal cat
begins to play with it own ghost.

7.

*(Via Badoino Quintilio: an Alpino soldier lost in Russia.
Formerly: "The Way of the Broken Houses")*

1998.

Came Badoino's very old sister
came Clemé with figs
came Rina with rabbits' ears
came Bruno with scissors
came Enzo with *motorino*
came Mrs. Maiocchi, first time for
   20 years out of the house,
came with her white hands
came the Englishwoman from out
   of the golden cage
a little shaken by the antennae –
came the Mayor, spit, spit
came the priest, always the priest
& the band made up for the occasion
rusty but trumpeting
all coming, all shouting
   Badoino!, Badoino!

8.
Susanna is walking down to the piazza
and I am holding a bucket of sheets.
Stai facendo la biancheria? Come sei bravo!
I unlock the gate and climb to Marilena's
whose terrace looks over the roofs of the village.
I drape the white sheets over the railings
and then look casually across the valley
it's as if someone's handed me the world..!

Serreta

Across the valley lies *Serreta*.
It is perfect, with its red roofs,
its spired church, its emptiness.

Better to leave it across the valley.
Walking towards it the vision fades,
we are too close, lack perspective...

The houses are rotting, and the dogs
let us not talk about the dogs
that would have mouthfuls out of us...

And the few people who live there
are surely ghosts, they hide
behind shutters, they hardly move.

Now that we are here we cannot see.
We are being suffocated by the air.
I would hate to die here in *Serreta*.

Riviera

We hid under the tunnel in *Via Milano*
to escape from the thunder
and the whiplash of lightning and rain.
Just three chairs holding the water back.

And then the slow climb into the hills
the wipers playing their music of nerves,
the olives sluiced, cleansed, waiting
for that hot god that comes after storms...

The lightning weaker now, less frequent
distant lights leaning on the villages:
Calderina, Castello, Serreta, Gorleri
suddenly broadened and held by arrows of mauve

before the folding in of shuttered rooms
dark, tense, moody spaces
the bloated icon, *la noia,* bitterness
the fruit that's always lusty in the mouth...

Rina's War

Lombardy '43. Fog lingers with fog
and the silent progress of bicycles
has swallowed the wail of sirens.

Rina cannot see the Germans
and the Germans cannot see Rina.
All is lost in the perfection of fog.

Just as the blind can hear the light
Rina cycles off through the rice fields
aware of the butcher, the baker,

the priest, the collaborator, their
silent vehicles swishing past
under the shadow of their breath.

At the end of the fog was fog
and a landscape of ghostly bicycles
all ducking and weaving, all hoping.

For nearly two years Rina sliced
through Lombardy with never a collision.
Then suddenly the fog lifted.

Octopus

We were just two young people
in a hot city
making baby under the blue sky.

You were down at the fishmarket
gathering an octopus
which you scrubbed and cooked
I had to eat,
the octopus dripping off my chin.

Ah baby, baby...

Orange

And later when we moved across the city
we found ourselves walking through oranges
rotting oranges, careless oranges
which were here and there, which were everywhere
and you were saying *You know, I'm going to have that baby.*

From Boyton to Hollesley

The only time
I saw my Italian wife
riding a bicycle
was that summer in Boyton.
The roads were sweltering
in August mists
there were poppies on the wayside
and whilst I was thinking
my wife-with-child is
going to fall off and die
on this flat and
forsaken stretch of England
my wife was practising
this strange new tongue

But oh look at the rabbits
they are small and sweetish

they are quick and young..!

Stucco

I was your drunken Saxon
in your pretty Italian labyrinth

and when I sat on your doorstep of marble
you slapped my face and kissed me

but not necessarily in that order
and we agreed to hang around together

among the gifts of dogs and the *stucco*
the debris of mercantile grandeur

and now all you give me are snatches
of sleep and a tribe of children

who have come screaming out of history
with such fluted lyrical voices.

Camogli

As if picking nits
out of the cauldron of the earth

Cristina, Jack and William
sit on the banked edge of the surf

choosing stones and crystals
out of the fish-stubble of *Camogli:*

tokens of green, smooth blues
the sudden rush of diamond

a piece of terracotta
fused with delicate ceramics

the great design of the sea
broken into bits, collectable.

The Backwater

For five years sitting against
a tree next to the river
with the sea over the mountains
is not really what happened.

Moving house was more our line.
Each time leaving a longer
climb of stairs and a confederacy
of life-sucking landlords.

The years passed.

A small boy ran into the bedroom
and announced that he was mine.

Later there was a marriage
with feasting.

But the problem was Greenbacks,
Deutschmarks, Soldi, *palanche*
such a knee-weakening lack.

So we dreamed of escape…

Life was the anxious study
of time-tables. Life was
a train leaving without us.

The Cloth

Behind the cloth was the world.
We could hear it murmuring like
a beast in the heat of the night
when not to sleep is perpetual pain.
Behind the cloth a thousand flickering
eyes were flickering in unsurprise.
On our quiet side of the cloth
we hoped that the blood-curdling world
would pass us by, would let us sail
to some unspectacular, unwanted isle.
With all our might we heard the waters
lapping at our heavy bed, becalmed
in a voyage of privations, humiliations.
Then – glory to God – the winds came
and the cloth leapt against the window,
we could feel the bed slicing through
the sea, our hearts a little less dry.
And for a second the cloth was sucked
out into the night and all of a sudden
we had a vision of what was behind.

Art Gallery

Others have bored me.
This one quickly had our clothes off.
There was too much in it

ordering nudity.
Even the woman at the door winked
loosening the buttons on your shirt.

Proceed this way for a Caravaggio
and remember art is an aphrodisiac.
The sun beat hot on the back of our necks,

stripped to the waist
we studied our first St. Francis.
A young man with a glove whispered

I did not catch his words
a Latin tongue slips back into its mouth,
a round Venus touches the top of her thigh

opens her legs, yawns.
An old flea tries to escape –
gets caught in the brushwork

we kiss under a Bacchus
thinking the same thought.
Stern civic dignitaries observe.

Rina the Afflicted

Two years ago, dear Rina, you
came to stay and spent the first hour
flailing at the bottom of the stairs.
So I carried squeezed orange juice
to your lips for several days
and heard such soft cries:
Gentilezza!, che gentilezza!
The house swayed with your dolours
and sometimes a star dropped

out of the sky. Now you're with us again,
seized by arthritic devils.
I see you lying across the armchair,
your legs somehow pointing
in the wrong direction, rather like
a medieval picture of sloth.
Even the door is suffering.
And I can hear the words *Aiuto!, aiuto!*
walking away from your lips.

I was born

I was born in a Chinese restaurant,
I soon learnt the art of being quick.
The pleasures of *Dim Sum* were revealed,
I learnt the management of rice
the thin athleticism of the chop stick.

Soon I was a grandmother.

When I died I was rich enough.
I could hear the prayers of my loved ones
beating their wings in a warm temple.
Life is as quick as the pouring of tea.

I advise you therefore to run your hands
over its swiftness, in the quiet of an afternoon
where the streets of the city converge:
when nobody's listening, watching

weeping, or gnashing their teeth.

The Song of the Clock

Friend, accomplice, let us drink to our respective ends
now that we have the strength to raise a glass to our lips,

now that we are clothed against that secret ticking clock.
With wine on our lips, let us try to imagine ourselves

laid out, naked, on the cold marble slab of our final bed,
our restaurant bills unpaid and ever unpayable.

Friend, more ice? Shall we dilute our rented pleasures?

The Jacket

You put on a jacket for the doctor.
The doctor won't even see it. He will ask
you to take it off. The doctor prefers
naked bodies. It makes his work easier.

He will put his hand into your stomach,
reach up through those crowded lands and
nudge a faint heart into its proper orbit.
The doctor likes to be a little severe.

He doesn't give a damn about jackets.

The Carriage

I saw the death-carriage on the edge of the park,
it was made of glass and was exquisite.

Several well-placed jewels gave it a little sparkle.
Anyone could try it out, climb in, relax.

I said to Rina *This would be a fine way of seeing London.*
She gave me one of her wise smiles,

smoothed her frock and clambered in.
She lay face upwards, *all her aches drifting away –*

Then the coachman cracked his whip
and the white horses gathered a little pace

and the glass carriage glided like a sail-boat.
And people stopped, blew kisses, threw flowers,

never had Rina received so many bouquets,
she was drowning in flowers, like the forest...

The Corpse

When I looked at the sea
the blue-grey sea
it was my corpse I saw
floating gently under the waves.

I studied it, a little envious:
it was so peaceful, so laid-back.
As corpses go there wasn't much
wrong with it at all...

I wanted to wish it well
but my words fell on dead ears.
My corpse said nothing,
it was so valiantly discreet.

I watched it float
and then, in the way of the living,
I picked up a handful of stones
and tried to hit it.

Splash!, *splash!*: but my corpse
was not the easiest of targets.
Apart from a left foot
my rain of stones fell short.

So I watched it drift
out of harm's reach, stroked
and soothed by the soft sea.
Then I turned towards the bar.

Saint Anna's Funicular

When I go down to hell
I will take Saint Anna's funicular.
It will be waiting for me
in the nearly dark of a
velvet-skied Genoese evening.

I will be the only passenger
and the doors will slide shut
with a sublime finality.
It will be an extraordinary occasion,
this journey into eternity.

And in that narrow steep descent
I will be given my last vision
of the city against the sea
and I will pass lighted windows
full of comfort and chandeliers.

Padre Pio

(Canonisation, 1999)

It was like a curse.
This story of *Padre Pio*

following me across Europe
for nearly a decade

I could feel the hysteria
of the pages between my fingers

the awful vocabulary of eyes
the divine sweat…

Would it never be possible
to peep into a paper

without encountering
the fleshy glamour

of this peasant saint?
Well, all this passed away —

a mere ground swell
a kind of fevered titillation.

Padre Pio climbed
off the back pages

of the tabloids
kitsch, glossy, sandalled

and soared
into the light.

His jowls
articulate as wings.

God

When I want God
I ask the children to sleep

first they resist
too many things to do

the rats under the shed
need flushing out

should we take a cat?
Summer is eternal wakefulness

shall we muse on wakefulness?
But sleep always conquers,

they sleep, they breathe,
they breathe, they sleep

the morning comes...

Dictée

Do you remember Sonia's
dictation classes in the great hall?

The car that drove slowly
but surely along the pasture.

And all the university girls
pretty, pampered, lovely

and cheating... *Signorina*
Non si fa cosi durante gli esami!

and the sweat and the perfume
and the falling coils of perfect hair

and all those short journeys
Rapallo, Voltri, Nervi

and Sonia's gift –
what *was* Sonia's gift?

Ballo

Enzo has ducked down with the grass cutter.
Izio, the electrician, has gone Hawaiian.
Marilena, rich in houses, has beautiful hair.

The lady from Milan doesn't like *negri*
but she likes the strange vacuum of August
and she believes in the power of prayer.

Susanna in Venice since '68 –
her son is dancing with the thin blond girlfriend.
Sie sprechen Deutsch in piazza.

The old men are smoking like Turks
and always shouting, *Pino* is hawking his *Olivetti.*
No space for hiatus in dialect.

The blackshirt is gangly with cropped hair,
he is wearing braces with the faces of the *Duce,*
he is teaching his son how to tango.

My sad wife is ladling out sangria
and taking money for the *ballo, ah the ballo..!*
Clemé is spilling figs from her pockets.

And there's *Bruno* the rabbit catcher,
the barber, the olive-bottler,
the voyager, gerontion ball-breaker…

My wife is *daunsinge* with *Izio*
gliding round and round and round the *ballo*
I am watching his hand on her arse.

After the *ballo* we stack the chairs, tables
and take a car to the sea; we strip and swim.
And because it is dark we are laughing.

After Lutyens

I want to bathe your feet
with my tears

and then dry them
with my hair.

It is true
I do not have much hair

but then
your feet are so small.

Cara Mia

Now you can scold me in two languages
I think of a time when pleasures
were often more silent:
narrow streets leading without strife
to high-ceilinged rooms, hot skies
beckoning rain and clothes
lying strewn on marble floors waiting
voicelessly for the coming light.